SPACE CRUSADERS

Carl Sagan

Celebrated Cosmos Scholar

Rebecca Felix

Checkerboard Library

An Imprint of Abdo Publishing
abdobooks.com

ABDOBOOKS.COM

Published by Abdo Publishing, a division of ABDO, PO Box 398166, Minneapolis, Minnesota 55439.

Printed in the United States of America, North Mankato, Minnesota
102018
012019

Design: Kelly Doudna, Mighty Media, Inc.
Production: Mighty Media, Inc.
Editor: Liz Salzmann
Front Cover Photographs: Alamy (right), Shutterstock (left)
Back Cover Photographs: NASA (Aldrin, ISS, space shuttle, Apollo rocket), Shutterstock (planets)
Interior Photographs: Alamy, p. 15; AP Images, pp. 5, 17 (bottom left), 25, 27, 29 (top); Everett Collection NYC, p. 19; Getty Images, pp. 9, 11; NASA, pp. 13, 21, 29 (bottom left); PBS/Everett Collection, p. 23; Shutterstock, pp. 7, 17 (top center, top right, bottom center, bottom right); Wikimedia Commons, pp. 17 (top left), 28 (top), 29 (bottom right); Woodmiser/ Wikimedia Commons, pp. 8, 28 (bottom)

Library of Congress Control Number: 2018948530

Publisher's Cataloging-in-Publication Data
Names: Felix, Rebecca, author.
Title: Carl Sagan: celebrated cosmos scholar / by Rebecca Felix.
Other title: Celebrated cosmos scholar
Description: Minneapolis, Minnesota : Abdo Publishing, 2019 | Series: Space crusaders | Includes online resources and index.
Identifiers: ISBN 9781532117053 (lib. bdg.) | ISBN 9781532159893 (ebook)
Subjects: LCSH: Sagan, Carl, 1934-1996--Juvenile literature. | Astronomers--United States--Biography--Juvenile literature. | Cosmology--Juvenile literature. | Human contacts with extraterrestrial beings--Juvenile literature.
Classification: DDC 629.450 [B]--dc23

Contents

1

Skilled Space Enthusiast

Carl Sagan was an **astrophysicist**, astronomer, and professor. He loved space and devoted his life to getting his students excited about it too. He was also fascinated by the possibility of extraterrestrial life. Sagan spent much time researching and discussing this topic.

Sagan shared his ideas outside the classroom too. He was a gifted science writer who published more than 600 papers and articles and more than 20 books. Of these books, ***Cosmos*** was the most popular. It was published as a companion to Sagan's 1980 television series of the same name.

The TV series *Cosmos* is one of Sagan's best-known **legacies**. It remains the most-watched series in the history of public television. In the series, Sagan captured the attention of millions of viewers around the world and got them excited about space.

Sagan had great skill in explaining advanced science topics in a simple and interesting way. He became famous for making space and science popular with the public. His work also inspired several generations of scientists and explorers.

2 Excited about Stars

Carl Edward Sagan was born on November 9, 1934, in Brooklyn, New York. His parents were Sam and Rachel. Carl had one sister, Carol.

The Sagans lived in an apartment near the Atlantic Ocean. Coney Island was nearby, and the family visited the coastal neighborhood often. Carl and Carol would play on the beach.

Carl's parents read and had lively discussions about politics. Sam and Rachel also encouraged their children to study and read. Carl liked to read science fiction stories. He was especially interested in stories where people claimed to have seen **UFOs** or extraterrestrial life.

When he was about five years old, Carl's interest turned to the stars. He wondered what they were made of. Rachel sent her son to the library to find out.

Carl read a book about stars and learned that the sun is a star. He also began to realize how big the universe is. This early experience with space research influenced Carl's future.

Young Carl often asked his parents, friends, family, and neighbors in New York City what they thought stars were.

3

World's Fair Influence

Space had captured Carl's attention. After first reading about stars in the library, he continued to learn all he could about space. This included visiting Hayden **Planetarium** in New York. The displays taught Carl more about **galaxies**.

These planetarium visits shaped his future. So did another experience around the same time. Carl's parents took him to the New York World's Fair of 1939 to 1940.

Carl was amazed by what he saw at the fair. There were inventions everywhere! The creators shared visions of highways, robots, and more. It was at the fair that Carl saw a television for the first time.

The fair made Carl realize the world held wonders he never could have imagined. The inventions he saw showed him how science could be used in everyday life. Carl was inspired to continue his own scientific research.

Carl collected World's Fair items for many years after his visit.

A robot named Elektro at the 1939 World's Fair conducts musician Lois Kendall as she plays the double bass.

4 Eager Scholar

Sagan's enthusiasm for study and research served him well at school. In 1951, he graduated from high school early, at the age of 16. Sagan then moved to Chicago, Illinois. He studied **physics** at the University of Chicago.

Sagan's fascination with space continued in college. In addition to physics, he studied the planets and solar system. He also became interested in the search for extraterrestrial life. Sagan began researching the origins of life on Earth as well. These areas of study would remain Sagan's focus for much of his life.

In 1955, Sagan earned a **bachelor's degree** in physics. He remained at the University of Chicago and earned a **master's degree** in physics the next year. Sagan continued his education for three more years. In 1960, he earned a **PhD** in astronomy and **astrophysics**.

To earn his PhD, Sagan wrote a paper about the atmosphere on Venus. Research showed there was a lot of **carbon dioxide** in Venus' atmosphere. Sagan suggested that the carbon dioxide traps the sun's heat near the planet's surface. This is called the

Much of Sagan's research in college involved reading and writing. But he also performed science experiments.

greenhouse gas effect. Sagan believed the greenhouse gas effect would cause the planet to be much hotter than expected.

Sagan also believed the greenhouse gas effect could occur on Earth. He suggested that it could be caused by human activity releasing **carbon dioxide** into the atmosphere.

In recent years, rising global temperatures have been linked to human activities such as burning **fossil fuels**. These activities release carbon dioxide. This global warming is also called **climate change**. Sagan was one of the first scientists to **predict** climate change on Earth.

After completing his **PhD**, Sagan's time as a student was done. However, his work in research was not. Sagan became an astronomy researcher at the University of California in Berkeley. Sagan and his team worked with **NASA** to develop a special tool for its robotic **probes**. This would be the first of Sagan's many contributions to space exploration.

In 1962, Sagan moved across the country to Massachusetts. For the next six years, he worked at the Smithsonian **Astrophysical** Observatory in Cambridge. Sagan's work there would soon make him a nationally known scientist.

Sagan worked with NASA to build the probe *Mariner 2*. The probe went to Venus in 1962 and measured the surface temperature of the planet. The data proved Sagan's greenhouse gas effect theory!

5 The Search for ETs

At the observatory, Sagan studied the planets, focusing on Venus and Jupiter. During this time, he appeared on a television show about Venus. Sagan's appearance was well received. Viewers were impressed by his knowledge of and enthusiasm about the planet.

As Sagan learned more about the solar system, his interest in searching for extraterrestrial life increased. This search became his lifelong mission. He later revealed the possibility of extraterrestrial beings had fascinated him since childhood.

The possible existence of aliens had also long captured the interest of the public. But few scientists gave the idea credit. In fact, Sagan's focus on searching for aliens was **controversial**. Many scientists thought the idea of extraterrestrials was impossible or make-believe. They felt no true scientist should spend his or her time on the subject.

Even so, Sagan was not the first scientist to search for alien life. When he began his search, Sagan studied the work of others who had researched before him. He built on their work and pushed it further.

Sagan once said, "Are we an exceptionally unlikely accident or is the universe brimming over with intelligence?"

Sagan pointed to three conditions that suggested extraterrestrial life was possible. The first was the many places for extraterrestrial life to exist. Scientists had determined Earth's

galaxy was huge. And it is only one of a possible 100 billion galaxies in the universe! So, there were many possible places for aliens to live.

The next condition was the abundance of organic matter in the universe. Organic matter makes up air, plants, and other things plants and animals need to survive. Organic matter is found on other planets, on meteors, and even in the areas between stars. "The stuff of life is everywhere" in space, Sagan said.

Time was the final condition Sagan used to argue the possibility of alien life. Life on Earth began with bacteria and other single-celled organisms. Over billions of years, these life-forms **evolved** into plants and animals, including humans. Some areas of the solar system are even older than Earth. This means evolution could have occurred elsewhere in the solar system as it did on Earth.

Sagan said the combination of these three conditions made it unlikely that Earth was the only planet that could support life. He believed there may be millions of civilizations in our galaxy alone! Sagan would spend the rest of his career studying this possibility.

CELESTIAL SCHOLARS

NICOLAUS COPERNICUS (1473–1543)

- Polish astronomer
- First to realize that Earth and other planets orbit the sun
- Key figure of the Scientific Revolution, a series of events that shaped modern science

GALILEO GALILEI (1564–1642)

- Italian scientist, mathematician, and philosopher
- First to use telescopes to study the night sky
- Pioneered study of the cosmos

STEPHEN HAWKING (1942–2018)

- British physicist and cosmologist
- Wrote several books on theories of space and time
- Famous for his predictions and study of black holes

JOCELYN BELL BURNELL (1943–)

- British astrophysicist
- Discovered a new type of star called a pulsar
- First female president of the Institute of Physics

NEIL DEGRASSE TYSON (1958–)

- American astrophysicist and science educator
- Director of the Hayden Planetarium
- Host of 2014 *Cosmos* series

ELON MUSK (1971–)

- South African engineer and space enthusiast
- Founder of SpaceX, a spacecraft manufacturer and space exploration company
- Dreams of starting a human colony on Mars

6 Extraterrestrial Adviser

Due to his work on the search for extraterrestrial life, Sagan was considered a pioneer of exobiology. This is the study of life in space and on planets other than Earth. This field is also called astrobiology.

People took note of Sagan's excitement about and knowledge of space. He had a talent for communicating space topics in a way that was easy to understand. Fellow scientists and scientific organizations would ask Sagan to speak to the public about space. He became a point of contact between the scientific community and the public.

Sagan continued to spread his ideas about space exploration and the possibility of extraterrestrial life. In 1966, Sagan put his ideas into writing in his book *Intelligent Life in the Universe*. He was also an adviser on the 1968 film *2001: A Space Odyssey*. The movie is about astronauts traveling to Jupiter in a spaceship controlled by artificial intelligence.

STELLAR!

Russian astronomer Gavriil Adrianovich Tikhov was the first person to use the term *astrobiology*. He wrote a book titled *Astrobiology* that was published in 1953.

Sagan advised filmmakers to suggest, but not show, the existence of extraterrestrial life in *2001: A Space Odyssey*. He said showing an imaginary alien race would create "an element of falseness" in the movie.

7 Professor and Probes

In 1968, Sagan became director of the Laboratory for Planetary Studies at Cornell University in Ithaca, New York. Three years later, he became a professor at the university. He also continued to work on projects for **NASA**.

Sagan urged NASA to explore farther into space. He helped design NASA's *Viking 1* and *Viking 2* **probes**. Their mission was to land on Mars. They launched in 1975 and took nearly a year to reach Mars. The probes then sent back the world's first photos of the planet.

In 1977, NASA launched probes *Voyager 1* and *Voyager 2*. They were sent into the outer solar system. These probes had sound recorders and cameras to capture data about space.

Sagan lead a team that created special gold plates for each *Voyager* probe to carry. The plates contain information about Earth and its people. Sagan's team hoped that if extraterrestrial beings existed and found one of these plates, they would learn about Earth. *Voyager 1* and *Voyager 2* still travel in space today.

The *Viking* and *Voyager* probes were of great interest to the public. Sagan's talent for explaining topics related to space

Before launching the *Viking* probes, Sagan and the NASA team tested models of the probes in Death Valley, California.

and astronomy often drew reporters to him. Sagan became a spokesperson for space exploration. He was a guest on television and radio talk shows and soon became famous.

8 Cosmos

Sagan spoke about space to many different groups, including the US Congress. He urged Congress to support programs working to determine whether humans could live on Venus. Some people found Sagan's ideas unbelievable or **controversial**. But this only increased the attention he received. Sagan's success as an author also played a part in his popularity. By 1979, he had published six books about space.

In 1980, Sagan began regularly sharing his space knowledge on television. Sagan and Ann Druyan wrote a television series called ***Cosmos***. Druyan was a science communications specialist. She and Sagan had worked together on the *Voyager* project.

Cosmos consists of 13 one-hour **episodes**. On the show, Sagan discusses the history of the universe, the origins of life on Earth, and future space exploration. *Cosmos* aired in 60 countries, reaching millions of viewers. And it was an instant hit!

Sagan released a companion book to *Cosmos* the same year. It was on many best-seller lists for more than a year. Historians believe the show and book made Sagan the most famous US scientist in the world during the 1980s.

Cosmos became one of the most successful shows on PBS television. The network's 1982 poster promoting many of its shows highlights Sagan's contribution.

9 Honors and Health

Amid his *Cosmos* success, Sagan began another venture. He co-founded an international organization called the Planetary Society. Its mission is to inspire and inform the public about space and space exploration. Today, it is one of the largest space-interest groups in the world.

Sagan also continued to write. He published several more books in the 1980s and 1990s. All of Sagan's books were popular with the public. His 1985 novel *Contact* was made into a movie in 1997. It is about scientists trying to make contact with extraterrestrial life.

Sagan enjoyed many honors throughout his life. He received 22 honorary degrees from US colleges and universities. These degrees were in recognition of his contributions to science and education.

In 1977, he was awarded **NASA**'s Distinguished Public Service Medal. In 1994, he received the National Academy of Sciences' Public Welfare Medal. This award recognizes people who have used science to benefit the welfare of society.

Sagan remained a professor at Cornell until his death.

Also in 1994, Sagan received difficult news. He was **diagnosed** with bone marrow **cancer**. He was later further weakened by **pneumonia** and was unable to recover. Sagan died on December 20, 1996, at the age of 62.

10

Carrying On a Cosmic Legacy

Sagan's death was not the end of his influence. His teaching at Cornell had educated and inspired a new generation of scientists. Sagan's books and TV series have continued to educate the nonscientific community about space.

In 2006, **NASA's** Ames Research Center opened the Carl Sagan Center for the Study of Life in the **Cosmos**. The Mountain View, California, site has three laboratories, a public exhibition area, and a theater. Research teams there continue Sagan's search for extraterrestrial life.

Sagan is also remembered for pushing boundaries. Many people believe Sagan's ideas helped push space exploration into new areas. Though he inspired many, some thought his ideas were **controversial**. His supporters point out that many discoveries about space have started with these kinds of imaginative ideas.

Astrophysicist Neil deGrasse Tyson is an enthusiastic supporter of Sagan's work and ideas. In 2014, Tyson honored Sagan by hosting a follow-up to Sagan's *Cosmos* television series.

Druyan (*left*) and Tyson (*right*) worked together on Cosmos: *A Spacetime Odyssey*.

It is called ***Cosmos****: A Spacetime Odyssey*. The show increased many people's wonder of space, keeping Sagan's **legacy** alive.

Timeline

1934

Carl Edward Sagan is born on November 9 in Brooklyn, New York.

1951

Carl graduates from high school early and begins college at the University of Chicago.

1939–40

Carl's parents take him to the New York World's Fair. Exhibits at the fair influence Carl's ideas about science and everyday life.

1955–1960

Sagan earns a bachelor's degree in physics, a master's degree in physics, and a PhD in astronomy and astrophysics.

1962

Sagan begins working at the Smithsonian Astrophysical Observatory in Cambridge, Massachusetts.

1968

Sagan becomes director of Cornell's Laboratory for Planetary Studies.

1971

Sagan becomes a professor at Cornell, a position he holds for the rest of his life.

1977

Sagan receives NASA's Distinguished Public Service Medal.

1980

Sagan publishes the book *Cosmos* and hosts a TV series of the same name.

1996

Sagan dies on December 20 at the age of 62.

Glossary

astrophysics—a branch of astronomy. Astrophysics is the study of the behavior and measurements of objects outside Earth's atmosphere. Someone who works in astrophysics is an astrophysicist.

bachelor's degree—a college degree that is usually earned after four years of study.

cancer—any of a group of often deadly diseases marked by harmful changes in the normal growth of cells. Cancer can spread and destroy healthy tissues and organs.

carbon dioxide—a heavy, colorless gas that is formed when fuel containing the element carbon is burned.

climate change—a long-term change in Earth's climate.

controversial—of or relating to a discussion marked by strongly different views.

cosmos—the universe.

diagnose—to recognize something, such as a disease, by signs, symptoms, or tests.

episode—one show in a television series.

evolve—to develop gradually. This process is evolution.

fossil fuel—a fuel formed in the earth from the remains of plants or animals. Coal, oil, and natural gas are fossil fuels.

galaxy—a very large group of stars, planets and other objects in space.

greenhouse gas—a gas, such as carbon dioxide, that traps heat in Earth's atmosphere.

legacy—something important or meaningful handed down from previous generations or from the past.

master's degree—a college degree that is usually earned after one or two years of additional study following a bachelor's degree.

NASA—National Aeronautics and Space Administration. NASA is a US government agency that manages the nation's space program and conducts flight research.

PhD—doctor of philosophy. Usually, this is the highest degree a student can earn.

physics—a science that studies matter and energy and how they interact.

planetarium—a building or room in which images of stars, planets, and other space objects are shown on a high, curved ceiling.

pneumonia (nu-MOH-nyuh)—a disease that affects the lungs. It may cause fever, coughing, or difficulty breathing.

predict—to guess something ahead of time on the basis of observation, experience, or reasoning.

probe—a device used to explore and send back information.

UFO—unidentified flying object. A flying object in the sky that some people believe could be a spaceship from another planet.

ONLINE RESOURCES

To learn more about Carl Sagan, visit **abdobooklinks.com**. These links are routinely monitored and updated to provide the most current information available.

Index

MORRIS AUTOMATED INFORMATION NETWORK
0 1009 0116231 1